Charm
CASTING

Rebecca-Anuwen

Cover photo by Catherine Berry
www.entirelycatherinephotography.com

Design by GW Illustration
www.GrantWickham.co.uk

 RebeccaAnuwen.com

 facebook.com/YourSherosJourney

 instagram.com/YourSherosJourney

Visit: www.RebeccaAnuwen.com/the-shop for ready made charm
casting sets

Contents

Welcome

I'm delighted that you're here and ready to learn more about Charm Casting.

There are no firm rules here. You can read through each section in the order outlined in this book (which I'd recommend if you're completely new to Charm Casting). Or, alternatively, jump straight to the area that intrigues you the most.

All you need to do is show up with a sense of wonder and curiosity. Then get ready to have some fun as you decipher the language of your soul.

Before You Begin

Why Cast Charms?

In this book, we'll explore the practice of Charm Casting. This powerful form of divination uses small charms and trinkets that you cast upon a surface to connect with your inner wisdom.

Charm Casting is powerful in its simplicity.

In fact, I believe that its power comes from the fact that there are no rules. Well... there are a few guidelines – but really, you're free to do this however you please.

There's no formal guidebook in Charm Casting – or not in the usual sense, the way you'd have for a rune set or oracle deck, anyway. Yes, I'll give you some guidance in this book, but please take what works for you, and either adapt or 'throw out' the rest.

As you work through this book and learn more about the practice of Charm Casting, you'll find a new way to connect with your intuition and interpret its messages. You'll discover your own unique way to work with the charms. And you'll use them to gain a deeper understanding of the patterns and stories in your life and get guidance on how to move forward.

All you need are:

- Some charms, trinkets or small objects to cast
- A container to stir or shuffle them in
- A surface to 'cast' your charms onto

In practice, this could be as simple as using a few objects you have lying around the house as charms. You could just use your hands to 'shuffle' them (like you would with dice) and then cast them onto a table. After that, it can be time to connect with your inner wisdom and interpret whatever message the charms have for you.

Or, of course, you can make the whole process much more elaborate. You'll probably do exactly this as you go along. At its heart though, Charm Casting is a simple and intuitive practice. It's easy to add to your charm collection (and your method) once you have the basics down. But it's hard to move out of overwhelm if you start out making it too fancy and complicated.

So start simple. Simple is best.

Becoming Your Own
Charm Casting Oracle

I want to make this very clear: the charms you choose to work with are a tool.

Yes, they help you to decipher the messages of your soul. But the actual questions you seek to answer come from a deep place of knowing within yourself.

For example, you might KNOW something isn't right, or KNOW it needs to change, but not know exactly what or how. These questions are a nudge from your soul, and the charms you use will help you to translate your soul's language.

In other words, the charms are not magic. Instead, YOU are the magic. Charm Casting just helps you learn to interpret your own unique blend of that magic.

That said, charms are a fabulous tool, so it's important to collect ones that resonate with you. Look for charms that attract your attention and evoke a sense of connection.

You're about to create a relationship with your set of charms. And just like with any other relationship, the more you nurture and respect the relationship with your charms, the more fulfilling it will be.

You'll use your charms as a way to connect with your intuition, so you can hear the wisdom and messages of your soul.

When you do this, you'll discover what's important to you and what's not.

You'll learn how to uncover the words, dreams and stories that describe what you truly want.

You'll connect to the truth of who you are.

But YOU are the magic.

YOU are the oracle.

The charms are simply a tool to help you remember and access your wisdom.

Divination

Dictionary.com defines divination as:

Divination [div-uh-ney-shuh n.]
Noun
Perception by intuition; instinctive foresight.

As you begin Charm Casting, know that you're taking part in a practice with a long history.

Human beings have always looked for answers to life's great mysteries. Before the abundance of oracle cards and other divination tools available to us today, people looked for meaning in whatever was around them.

Some people would look to the clouds, the trees or even the dust to see what messages, patterns or symbols they could identify.

The Chinese read patterns on tortoise shells, which evolved into the hexagrams of the I Ching.

The Vikings consulted runestones.

The Egyptians used fire, water and oil scrying. They also interpreted dreams and consulted oracles who spoke to the gods.

Meanwhile, the Romans looked for omens in the behaviour and actions of birds. They believed that birds' flight patterns indicated the will of the gods. They also had more unpleasant divination practices that involved inspecting the entrails of sacrificed animals...

In fact, there aren't many things that human beings haven't used for divination!

Here's a list of some of the most common types:

- **Astrology:** divination by celestial bodies
- **Augury:** divination by the flight of birds, etc.
- **Bibliomancy:** divination by opening books (frequently, but not always, religious texts) at a random page
- **Cartomancy:** divination by cards (often tarot and oracle cards)
- **Cheiromancy/palmistry:** divination by palms
- **Gastromancy:** divination by crystal ball
- **Numerology:** divination by numbers
- **Oneiromancy:** divination by dreams
- **Osteomancy:** divination by pieces of bone
- **Rhabdomancy:** divination by rods
- **Runecasting/runic divination:** divination by runes
- **Scrying:** divination by reflective objects

Other, less common forms of divination include:

- using salt
- dropping melted lead into water
- observing lamp flames
- using shells, smoke, mirrors, wood and even cakes and bread!

Some of these methods have now infiltrated popular culture as superstitions.

For example, the superstition of a black cat crossing your path is using animal behaviour as a form of divination. Similarly, the tradition of making a wish while breaking the wishbone of a cooked chicken with your little finger originated in osteomancy.

Awakening Your Intuition

Charm Casting is a way of connecting to your intuition – your inner wisdom.

Everyone can access their intuition. Absolutely everyone. No exceptions.

Some people find connecting to their intuition easier than others do, but it's a skill that can be learnt and practised. And the more you practise, the easier it becomes.

You may doubt your intuition because its quiet whispers are drowned out by the doubts, fears and overwhelm of everyday life. It may also be hard to hear the voice of your intuition because you've long since forgotten how to truly trust yourself.

We've spent much of our lives hearing the world we live in try to convince us that other people know what we need better than we do. The quiet voices of our intuition get drowned out by our fast-paced lives and by instant gratification. They get overwhelmed by the constant stream of other people telling us what to do, how to behave and what's true.

Our current society rarely values the gifts of our intuitive selves.

Intuition can't be measured, so it isn't seen as productive. It's perceived as having less value than something that's tangible and provable. Intuition lies in the realms of the mysteries: that which can't be explained or rationalised. We've been taught to fear what we can't explain or control, yet our intuition is at once our greatest strength and our way to access our inner power. It helps us to navigate our inner landscapes, so we can navigate the outer landscapes with more grace, ease and flow.

As you work with your charms, you'll gain a deeper understanding of, and access to, your intuition. And just like with a muscle, the more you use it, the stronger your intuition becomes.

To start with, you may feel rusty. You may feel that you're doing it wrong. But the truth is that you can't get this wrong. In fact, many people who start working with their intuition find that the most difficult part is that there is no right or wrong way to do it.

We human beings love rules. We've been taught that rules keep us safe. And while many rules do exactly that, some can limit us – stifling our growth and expression. We live in a world that's governed by rules. We're taught that there's a right way and wrong way to do everything. We strive for success and we fear failure. We want to achieve. We value getting there quickly and directly, not having time to waste.

And intuition is almost the polar opposite of ALL these things.

There's no wrong way to access your intuition.

There are no hard and fast rules. There's guidance, yes, but it's only guidance.

We've grown accustomed to following the rules. We want to get things right and we're afraid to get them wrong.

But when you step into the mysteries, the home of your intuition, you're no longer governed by the same rules or structures. At first, that can feel confusing.

As you awaken your intuition, though – as you learn to trust your inner voice and interpret the language of your soul – you'll experience a greater sense of inner freedom. You'll feel more connected to your inner power. You'll feel more confident in who you are and how you show up in the world.

But to do this, you need to embrace the mysteries – the mysteries you were taught to fear, and may indeed once have feared. When you embrace those mysteries, you'll realise that they're where you actually hold your greatest strength. They're where your greatest source of confidence, courage and inner knowing lie.

Then, once you activate your intuition, you'll step into a world of learning to trust both yourself and the messages from your soul. When you can do this, you'll stop seeking external validation. You'll stop holding back because of fears and old conditioning.

Once you begin to trust yourself and your intuition, your whole life changes. You start making EVERY choice you face in a way that aligns with your soul purpose. You make it from a place of inner power and confidence – a place of knowing that you have your own back.

You develop a clarity and a confidence that you can face anything that comes your way. You start creating your life from a place of conscious alignment, rather than from habit.

There's no doubt that as you begin to awaken your intuition, your life will change. And it will change in a really wonderful, empowering way.

People think that charms will 'give you the answers'. The truth is that they'll actually help you to find your own answers. They'll help you to remember the power and wisdom that you've always had.

To quote Glinda the Good Witch from The Wizard of Oz: "You always had the power, my dear. You just had to learn it for yourself."

Charm Casting

What is Charm Casting?

As mentioned in the previous section, Charm Casting is a method of divination that uses charms or trinkets in the same way as other methods use cards, runes or tea leaves. In other words, Charm Casting uses charms as a tool to connect with your inner wisdom and access messages from it.

It's a great practice if you're looking to explore a topic or concern you have.

You can use it to ask focused questions.

You can also use it to find the story behind patterns that you find yourself repeating.

The power of this form of divination (and any others that don't rely on someone else's guidebook) is that you learn to connect deeply with your own intuition. You begin to trust your own inner wisdom.

The way specific charms land on your throwing surface brings forward the stories of your life. And those stories are based on YOUR experiences and what's true for you.

Charm Casting is a fun, simple, yet profound practice. It's a powerful way to remember what's important to you, what you want and what your innermost dreams and desires truly are.

It helps you to connect to the truth of who you are – who you always were, before the world told you who and what you should be.

Can Anyone Use Charm Casting?

YES! As we said in the previous section, absolutely anyone can use the process of Charm Casting to connect with their intuition.

Some people may find it easier to work with their intuition in this way, or have a natural affinity for it. But absolutely everyone can use this form of divination.

Again, all you need are the tools, an attitude of curiosity and an open mind.

And just like with any skill, the more you practise it, the easier and more natural it becomes.

At first, it may feel a bit slow or clunky as you look for the messages. But very quickly, you'll feel an inner knowing – a recognition – about the message your charms are conveying to you.

How to Interpret Messages When There's No Guidebook

If you're used to working with oracle cards, you're probably also used to looking to the guidebook to interpret the messages within each card.

Yes, as time goes by, you may find that you start to put your own unique twist on the card's meanings. But most often, people just draw a card and go straight to the guidebook.

There's nothing wrong with that way of interpreting messages – guidebooks can be a valuable source of wisdom. I want you to take your relationship with your intuition to the next level, though. Because the way the cards or charms communicate with you is what's important, not how they communicate with the author of the guidebook.

Without a guidebook, Charm Casting relies on the person throwing the charms to draw their own symbolism from each individual charm and how it's positioned.

NOTE: In my shop, www.RebeccaAnuwen.com/the-shop The SHEro Toolkit charms may seem to be an exception to this, since they come with an optional guidebook. This is because I curated the charms to supplement the SHEro Toolkit Oracle cards, which also contain simple symbols just like the charms. But I've always encouraged you to ignore the guidebook. When you remove it from play, you're left listening to your own intuition for the messages.

You always have to listen for what the symbolism means to you.

For example, the Bee charm may mean community, hive mind or the sweetness of honey to one person. Meanwhile, to another who's allergic to bee stings, it might clearly mean 'danger'. Neither of these interpretations is wrong. Both are perfect for the person receiving the message. Each person's individual inner wisdom understands their own experiences of life, so it knows which symbols to use to best communicate with them.

Again, this may seem slow or frustrating at first. Most of us are used to listening to other people, and deferring to the opinions of 'experts' we think have more knowledge than we do. This, after all, is exactly what referring to a guidebook involves!

But very quickly, you'll find that the more time you take to practise and listen with all of your senses, the clearer and faster the messages will come through.

You'll also become more confident with hearing and interpreting the messages from your inner wisdom. While those messages may sometimes be uncomfortable or not what you wanted to hear, you won't be at odds with them the way you might be with a guidebook. You'll be more able to accept them, because you'll know them to be true.

And slowly, you'll start to trust yourself and your wisdom again.

Getting Ready to Work
with Your Charms

Collecting Your Charms

You can use pretty much any charm, trinket or small object as a charm in your Charm Casting set.

Whatever you use, it'll need to be small and robust enough to be thrown around with the other objects in your set without damage. It will also need to be something that you can give a meaning to.

As you begin hunting for and gathering your charms, you'll start to notice all sorts of small objects and regard them differently.

Collect anything that draws your attention or that you're curious about. Just because you collect something, it doesn't mean you have to immediately include that thing in your set.

You may find something that catches your attention and save it. Then, weeks or months later, you'll suddenly feel clear on how to use it. Only at that point would you add it to your Charm Casting set.

This is a journey of (re)learning to trust yourself.

So if something makes you curious and you feel called to save it, do so.

In time, the things you gather will either make sense to you or you'll lose your sense of curiosity about them and know it's time to release them.

If you'd like some additional inspiration, visit www.RebeccaAnuwen.com/the-shop to view the various charm casting sets available.

Here are a few examples of suitable objects that you could use as you start to build or add to your Charm Casting kit.

- Acorns or other nuts
- Beads (be careful with perfectly round ones though: they may just roll away!)
- Buttons
- Coins
- Dice
- Dominos
- Keys
- Metal jewellery charms
- Metal Thimbles
- Old earrings or pieces of jewellery that you no longer need
- Pieces of wood
- Rings
- Seed pods
- Shells
- Small bones
- Small pinecones
- Stones
- Tumbled stone crystals or crystal chips

Storing Your Charms

The way you store your charms is entirely up to you.

However, the container you use reflects your relationship with your charms. Notice the quality of your readings if you treat them like treasured, sacred tools. Then notice the quality if you neglect them. For example, if you let them get all sticky or covered in dust, without giving them care or attention, how do you think this will affect your relationship with them?

You might also want to consider whether the way you store and care for your charms reflects the way you feel about your intuition and inner wisdom.

I keep my main set of charms in a box on my desk. This is because I use them frequently, and can just dip my hand into the box whenever I want clarity or guidance.

By contrast, I keep my SHEro Toolkit charms in their special pouch. The pouch either sits within my 'big' box of charms, or on my altar. I save this set for specific Charm Casting readings with the maps, using them only when I want to explore a question in a deeper way.

The most important thing about the way you store your charms is that it needs to encourage you to actually use them. When you use your charms, you create a deeper relationship with them. That's the only way they can support you in accessing your intuition.

So accessibility is a key factor in how you choose to store them.

Charms to Get You Started

To start with, you'll want about 8-12 charms in your set.

This number is likely to grow quickly, but it's easier to start with fewer of them while you're getting familiar with Charm Casting. Then, as you get more confident, you can add more (and more and more and more...) charms to your set.

Initially, you may want to include small items that represent concepts like:

- Action
- Challenges
- Change
- Communication
- Finances
- New beginnings
- Relationships
- Resting or slowing down
- Stopping
- Success
- Your home
- Yourself

These concepts give you a great place to start for interpreting your readings.

As your experience and confidence grow, you can then add more charms to get greater insight and explore the nuances of the messages that come through.

Connecting with Your Charms

Once you have your charms, you'll want to connect with them. This means getting to know their energy and starting to connect with how they might show up in messages for you.

Think of your charm set as being made up of individual characters. Each character has its own flavour that it brings to the wider community. Each brings its own medicine and knowledge.

At one time in your life, you may find yourself 'hanging out' with a particular part of your community. Then, when your life changes, you may move to a different part of the community. But if you need guidance, before you know whose advice to seek, you need to find out who's who in your new community.

And it's exactly the same with your charms.

When I first get new charms, I like to just spend time with them.

I'll find somewhere quiet, and I'll go through each new charm, one by one. I'll notice how they each feel in my hand. I'll look at them, hold them and notice their colours and textures. I'll put them on my desk where I'm working, and I'll regularly look at them there.

As they sit with me, I'll pay attention to any thoughts or feelings I have about them.

I may keep them on my desk for a just few minutes or for a few days, trusting whatever feels right (again: you can't get this wrong!)

And I may go through this process several times, depending on what feels right for me.

Setting the Scene to Throw Your Charms

Once you're familiar with your charms, you'll want to start working with them to get the answers you're after.

You don't have to do anything fancy, but it's useful to make sure you're present and grounded when you ask your questions. This way, you're more likely to get clear, grounded answers.

As you set the scene for your Charm Casting, you may also want to light a candle or call in a goddess or deity you work with. You can do both of these things, or neither. It's entirely up to you and what feels right for you and your practice.

But the most important thing is to take a moment to become present and get clear on the intention of the question you're about to ask.

Again: clear, focused intention is the key to a clear, focused answer.

It ensures that you're in the best place to receive the guidance you seek.

Reading Surface

Choose Your Reading Surface

Decide what you want to cast your charms onto.

You may wish to cast them onto a sacred mat, an altar cloth or a favourite or special piece of fabric.

If you choose the fabric, consider what will work best. What texture do you want? Will it be plain or patterned? To start with, you may not want anything that's overly patterned, as it may be distracting.

Next, consider what size you want the fabric piece to be. Choose the size carefully: you don't want it so big that the charms get 'lost', or so small that charms roll off the edges.

Alternatively, you may choose to cast your charms into a shallow-edged box or onto a serving tray, so that they stay in a defined area once you cast them. Maybe you could even decorate a favourite plate to cast them onto.

As another option, to create some structure in your reading, you can use the Charm Casting Maps at the back of this book, or design your own maps.

Or, finally, it's perfectly OK to just use a convenient tabletop.

The Areas of Your Reading Surface

When you cast your charms, trust your intuition to understand the message you receive.

Sometimes, you can make it easier to hear what your intuition is saying by bringing some structure into your reading.

To create that structure, you can divide your overall casting surface up into specific areas that represent different areas of your life or experience. Either just imagine the lines dividing up the areas, or actually physically create those lines. For example, if you're using a box or plate, you could draw in the lines, or use tape to mark them out. Or, if you're using cloth, you could embroider it or sew on different coloured fabrics to represent the different areas.

Here's an example of how that might look:

```
                  Stuck in a Mental Process

     Past              Present            Future


                     Material World

                       ( Key
     Mind              Themes )          Conscious

     Body                               Unconscious


                      Soul World




                     Weighed Down
```

Mapping the casting area

If you use this layout, you'll split your casting area as follows:

- **Three vertical sections**: Past, Present and Future
- **Top area**: Mind, Conscious and Material world
- **Bottom area**: Body, Unconscious and Soul world
- **Top outer edge**: Stuck in a mental process
- **Bottom outer edge**: Things weighing you down
- **Central area**: Key themes coming up for you

Charm Casting Maps

Using a Charm Casting Map is similar to using a set card spread with your oracle or tarot cards.

It's a great way to gain deeper insight into a topic.

I've designed the Charm Casting Maps to help you coach yourself through any query that you're facing in life right now. They allow you to take a deeper look at a subject or a question that's currently relevant in your life.

These maps can give you a different perspective and bring to your conscious mind any thoughts, feelings, habits or patterns that are holding you back. They can also help you to acknowledge any changes you need to make or actions you need to take. Maps can give you a greater insight into your chosen topic, allowing you to explore in more detail subject areas that you might have otherwise overlooked.

Maps are also a great tool to use when you need more information around a topic, especially when consciously thinking about that topic makes you feel blocked.

If you're facing a particular challenge in some areas of your life, maps can give you a broader perspective. They can help you to see the situation in a light that you hadn't considered before.

They can also help you to deepen the connection with your own dreams and desires, especially when you feel disconnected from what you really want in life.

Finally, Charm Casting Maps are great for taking a complicated issue and untangling its threads to find greater clarity and purpose in whatever next steps that you take.

You'll find three Charm Casting Maps at the back of this book. You can also make your own, using a sheet of paper and marking it out with various topics or areas of interest.

When you cast your charms onto a map, ask yourself:

- What section of the map did the charm land on?
- Does being closer to the centre or outer edge of an area symbolise anything to you?
- Does landing directly on one of the illustrations add to the meaning of the charm?
- What does it mean if a charm lands off the map? (See page 48 for more information on this).

Making Your Own Casting Surface

It's fun to make your own Charm Casting surface.

Whenever you make your own sacred tool, it will have special meaning and significance to you.

So making your own casting area will help you to deepen your connection to your own readings and intuition.

I mentioned above that you could make a casting mat out of fabric or from a box lid. The pictures on the following pages show casting surfaces I've made: one is a box lid, and the other is a shallow box file.

I like the box file best. When I've finished with it, I can put my casting maps inside, close the lid and everything is stored away neatly and tidily.

If you decide to create a casting surface, remember to show up with intention and presence as you create it. Consider what interests you and how you'd like to explore your answers more. When you do readings now, is there something missing from your answers? If so, find a way to include each of those things in your casting area.

You could include any, all, or none of the following things in a casting surface:

- Animals
- Areas of your life
- Compass Directions
- Crystals
- Days of the week
- Elements
- Herbs
- Months of the year
- Numbers
- Plants
- Seasons
- Trees
- 'Yes'/'No'
- Zodiac houses or signs

You could use different colours to represent different things, or use stickers, scrap paper, washi tape, illustrations, drawings, paintings, sewn objects and more.

The image below is the first throwing surface I ever made.

I decorated the entire lid with different types of washi tape. You can see I clearly marked the surface into three vertical areas, and a 'top' and 'bottom' of the surface.

I also used washi tape that represented the seasons and elements on the sides. So if I wanted a timescale for something, I would read the 'season' that the relevant charms landed next to.

There's also lots of imagery that adds another layer to the charms I cast in each reading.

I don't try to read everything on this surface with every charm. It's only there for guidance. Sometimes the imagery might seem important, while at other times it's the grid.

This is important: I don't fit my reading to the casting surface. Instead, I use the casting surface as a way to offer additional insight if I need it.

The second casting area is much simpler – mainly using the elements, represented by coloured paper, for guidance. But you can see there's still a clear 'top' and 'bottom' on the casting surface.

How to Use
Your Charms

Casting Your Charms

Now you're ready to cast your charms!

This will require some practice until it feels completely natural.

You want the charms to flow freely and distribute themselves nicely over your casting area – not too spread out from each other, but not in one big lump either.

Practise casting with varying speeds and levels of force, and casting from different heights and in different directions. Keep experimenting until you find a combination that feels just right for you.

If you have a small number of charms, you may want to simply pick them up and cast them from your hand. Perhaps try rolling them from your palm, or something more like a 'drop' from your fingers. Or, if you've stored them in a bag, bowl or small basket, you may want to cast them directly from their container.

Alternatively, if you have a large box of charms, you may want to move your fingers through whatever container you've stored them in. Perhaps stir them a little, then scoop out as many as feels right for you (one or two, or a handful) and cast them from your hand.

Simple Charm Draw

Another way to use your charms is to draw a single charm from the container.

I've mentioned that my box of charms always sits on my desk with me. As I work through the day, I might find myself with a question. If an answer doesn't immediately come to mind, I gently move my fingers through my box of charms, and draw out just one charm (or sometimes a couple) for some quick guidance.

This practice is powerful in its simplicity.

It's something you can do anytime and anywhere.

And it's a quick, easy way to gain insight when you need it most.

Once you've drawn your charm, notice how you feel when you see it. Become aware of any instant feelings, thoughts or messages. Notice – in other words – what you notice. Then make a note of your initial thoughts and feelings about the charm.

This will give you great insight into the answer you seek.

Sometimes I draw one charm, and then draw an additional one or more for clarification. Just remember that this is supposed to be a quick, easy draw. Don't overcomplicate it. Trust your first instincts, and don't overthink it.

Your first answer is often the right one.

Drawing a 'Charm of the Day'

This practice is exactly what it sounds like: you draw a single charm each day.

You may wish to do this to deepen your knowledge of and connection with your intuition, and get a better understanding of how your soul talks to you.

You can also draw a daily charm to ask for general guidance on the day ahead.

Whichever charm you draw, make a note of it. Note down its meaning to you, how you felt about it and anything about it that stood out for you. Then, throughout the day, check in to see how the charm's message and your thoughts about it resonate with your experiences of the day.

Once you've been doing this for a period of time, you'll start to notice themes and patterns emerging. You may find that certain charms have certain meanings for you. Perhaps you'll notice that when they come up, they're – as I heard Molly Remer once say – a 'cosmic wink' from the Universe. One might tell you that you're on the right track, and that everything is going to be OK. Another might turn out to be a definite "Whoah! Stop right there!" warning sign.

Regardless, choosing a charm each day is a powerful way to connect with your charms and deepen your relationship with them and with your intuition.

Interpreting
the Messages

Some Charm Meanings to Get You Started

This is a list of potential meanings for charms. I say 'potential meanings' because – as we've talked about above – your personal meaning for the charm or the message you get in the moment is what's important.

It's worth repeating: there IS no 'right' meaning for a charm.

Having said that, some charms do have a 'typical' meaning. Knowing these meanings can be a good place to start if you're feeling stuck. Here are a few of them:

- **Airplane:** Success, Taking off, Travel, Dreaming, Sky high
- **Apple:** Wisdom, Knowledge
- **Arrow:** Direct action, Getting straight to the point (it may also point at something significant, for example, at another charm or at an area or image on the casting surface)
- **Bed:** Need to rest
- **Belt:** Restrictions, The need to tighten your belt, Holding things together
- **Boat:** Smooth sailing, Flow, Travel
- **Butterfly:** Change, Transformation
- **Car:** The direction you're taking your life
- **Castle:** Home, Strong boundaries, Being too protective
- **Clock:** Time limit, Resources
- **Coins:** Abundance, Sum of money, Receiving gifts
- **Cup:** Receiving, Filling yourself up
- **Dog:** Loyalty, Companionship
- **Heart:** Passion, Love, Relationships

- **Horseshoe:** Luck, Bad luck, Superstitions, Old tales
- **Fan:** Hiding something, Concealing
- **Flowers:** Beauty, Gifts, Abundance
- **Grapes:** Abundance
- **Handcuffs:** Stopping, Thinking before you act
- **Jigsaw Piece:** Mystery, Only part of the issue or solution
- **Lightbulb:** Ideas, Inspiration
- **Pen:** Commitment, Journaling, Creativity
- **Rings:** Commitment, Relationship
- **Rosette:** Success, Winning, Positive outcome
- **Shoes:** Moving forward, Starting something new
- **Skull:** Ancestors, Spirits
- **Snake:** Transformation, Inner power
- **Tortoise:** Slowing down, Going slow and steady
- **Watering Can:** The need for nurturing and care

How to Interpret the Messages

Once you've thrown your charms, first look at the overall pattern they make and allow yourself to receive any messages from it.

Then notice your first response to the pattern: the feelings, emotions, sensations and maybe even memories it brings up.

Pay attention to any words or thoughts that enter your mind as you look at the pattern.

Look for any symbols or repeating patterns in the way the charms have fallen.

Where are they in relation to the throwing surface? Are some in the middle, at the edges or even off the surface altogether?

Let the pattern and placement tell you a story.

Next, look for any messages in the connections between individual charms. What overall scene do the connections create, and how does that relate to your question?

Are there any clusters of charms? Have some fallen on top of others?

Just notice what you become aware of.

Finally, once you have an overall feel for the patterns and connections, move your focus to the individual charms. What part of the message does each charm tell you?

Look at each charm, paying attention to its colour and texture. Then ask yourself:

- Are there any words? If so, what do they mean to you?
- Have any charms fallen upside-down (see the next page)?
- Are any of them hiding behind other charms?
- Have any charms joined together?
- Do any them point in a certain direction?

Allow your intuition to show you the deeper meanings.

Listen to your initial response to the charms – this is your intuition communicating with you. Again: your first response is almost always the most accurate.

Remember to trust your intuitive thoughts. Prioritise them as you interpret your charms – even if they say something different from each charm's traditional symbolic meaning.

Most importantly, have fun! Keep in mind that the charms are simply a tool to help you access your own intuitive wisdom. So you'll get out of them whatever you put in.

Face-Down Charms

If one or more of your cast charms lands face-down, it's up to you whether to give this meaning or not. Always follow your intuitive guidance.

Some charms don't have a 'front' and a 'back'. Others have clearly defined 'faces' or 'sides'.

So if one of your charms lands with its face down, you can simply turn it the correct way up and read it as you normally would. Or, alternatively, you can decide to see the reversal as more significant.

Here are some ideas about what a face-down charm could mean:

- You're hiding or ignoring the message of the charm
- The message is in your subconscious patterns, and needs bringing forward into your conscious awareness
- The message of the charm is leaving your life
- The message of the charm has a weak influence on you
- The message of the charm is a blockage in your life
- The message of the charm needs balancing in your life
- The message of the charm is an area of your life that needs your attention and some development
- The message of the charm represents something challenging for you
- The message of the charm represents an inner reflection of the external message

For example, let's say you cast an upright Crown, an upright 'Fearless,' a face-down Peacock, and a face-down first-place Rosette.

The two upside-down charms could mean that you're not owning your value, worth, contribution, skills or significance. They could also mean that you're hiding from showing up fully, taking up space or shining.

Or...

Alongside the Crown, these upside-down charms could mean that you're not owning your sovereignty and being 'fearless' in pursuing your dreams, standards or boundaries.

Or...

The reversed charms could indicate that you're not confidently or fully expressing yourself, your skills or your gifts.

Or...

The fact that the two charms are upside-down could have no meaning at all, and you could interpret them as if they'd landed face-up. In this case, the Peacock and Rosette might symbolise being proud of your achievements.

The only 'right' way to interpret them is the one that resonates with your inner wisdom.

Charms that 'Fall Off' the Throwing Area (AKA 'Jumping' Charms)

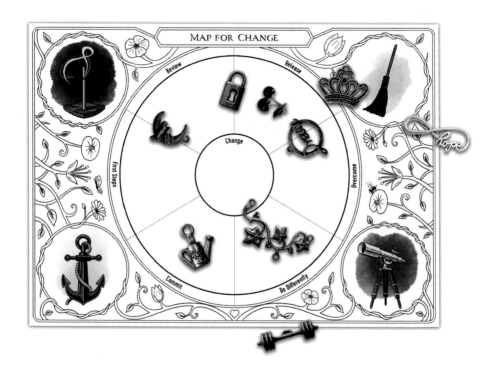

Just as oracle cards sometimes appear to 'jump' out of the deck, some charms can roll outside of the throwing area when you cast them.

They may fall outside of the map, or roll off your plate or your casting area.

You can choose to simply discard these charms as not relevant to your reading.

Or...

You can interpret the fact that they've fallen outside of your reading area as meaning that whatever they represent is actively irrelevant to your question.

Or...

You can interpret them in some other way that feels right for you. For example, a charm that falls outside your casting area could represent:

- Something that's outside of your conscious awareness right now
- Something that you aren't seeing clearly
- Something that isn't as important as you first thought
- Something that you're ignoring

In the Map for Change example above, you could dismiss the Infinity 'Hope' charm, the Dumbbell charm, and even the Crown charm from the reading.

Or...

You could interpret the Crown alongside the Broom. Perhaps it might mean sweeping out extravagant ways of expressing yourself that aren't yours. Or it might mean clearing the patterns so you can embody more of your own authority and sovereignty.

Or...

You could also see their message as saying that you're ignoring or dismissing your own hope, optimism, strength and resilience in the face of change.

The same is true for the charms on the casting mat below.

In this case, you could just ignore the Black charm (the New Moon). Or you could perhaps interpret it as you not owning your inner wisdom in times of significant challenge.

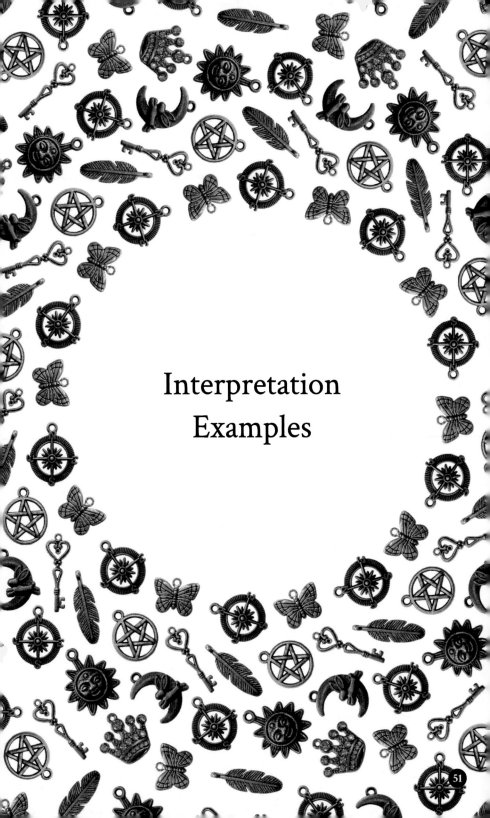

Interpretation
Examples

Interpretation Example 1:
Map for Change

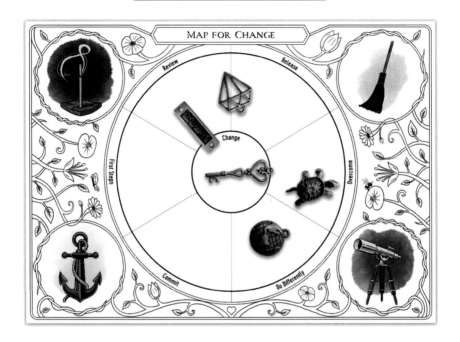

I created this map to use when you know you need to make some life changes, but you're not sure where to start. It will also help you to explore the possibilities for change.

The main areas of the map are:

- **Review:** charms that fall in this area indicate what you need to review before you can make your changes. All might not be as it seems, so you'll need to look at things in this area again to make sure everything is in order.

- **Release:** charms that fall in this area reflect things that you need to release in order to move on and make the changes you want.

- **Outcome:** charms that land in this area tell you a possible outcome if you go ahead and make the changes you want or need.

- **Do Differently:** charms here reflect what you need to do differently to make the changes you desire.
- **Commit:** charms here tell you what you need to commit to – not just think about, but truly commit to.
- **First Steps:** charms here reflect the first steps you need to take to build the momentum that will bring the change you want.

Initial thoughts on this reading:

Looking from a 'wide' perspective first, I notice two main things: the First Steps and Commit areas are empty, and the Key has landed right in the centre of the map.

One interpretation of this could be that the key to the change still isn't clear, so it's not yet time to commit to any action.

Looking closer:

The Key and 'Silence' are both the centre of the map. This might mean that now is the time to get clear on what you really want. You might need to spend time in silence and review what you want, as it might not be what you first thought.

'Silence' and the Diamond are both in the Review section. Perhaps this means you'll find your 'treasure' (the Diamond) once you realise what you need to let go of. And you'll realise this after a period of silent review and contemplation.

The Tortoise is in the Overcome section. This could be a message to go slow and steady – to recognise that this is a process you can't rush.

The World Globe has fallen in the Do Differently section. This could be an intuitive nudge to look at the stories you tell yourself. You might need to make a significant change – maybe to adopt a new world view or belief before you can move on.

Overall, this reading might suggest that you're making your choice from a place of habit, expectation or 'should'. Instead, you need to go back and review what you really want. Only when you're clear on your own choices will it be time to make any changes.

Interpretation Example 2:
Map for Clarity

I created the Map for Clarity to use when you're seeking greater clarity around a situation.

The map sections include:

- **Hidden:** charms that fall in this area of the map show you what's hidden from view, or what you may not have considered or seen.
- **Avoiding:** charms in this section reflect things that you've been avoiding or sabotaging. Once you have the clarity you seek, you'll probably need to make some kind of change in your life around these things.
- **Look Again:** charms in this area nudge you to take a closer look at whatever they represent, because things may not truly be as they first appear.

- **Clarity:** charms that fall in this section bring you more of the clarity you seek. They identify where to look for more clarity or what you need to do to experience it.

Initial thoughts on this reading:

Looking from a 'wide' perspective first, I again notice two main things. The Autumn Leaf is by itself in the Clarity section. Meanwhile, the rest of the charms cluster together in (or close to) the Avoiding section.

One interpretation of this could be that you're trying to avoid acknowledging that you already know what you want or need to do. And perhaps your reason for avoidance is that you know gaining clarity will involve change (Autumn Leaf).

Looking closer:

The Pumpkin has fallen on the centre line between Hidden and Avoiding. This could mean you're not owning your gifts or celebrating the fruits of your harvest. Maybe you're pretending that you don't already have the answers to the questions you seek.

The Garden and Crown both sit in the Avoiding section too. This could reflect that you're not owning your inner power and sovereignty over your 'garden' (which could reflect your land, your world, your body or your resources).

The Horseshoe has fallen between the Avoiding and Look Again sections. This might mean that you're leaving things to luck and just hoping that everything will turn out OK. You might instead need to take responsibility for actively, consciously creating and moving towards what you want.

The Boot is sitting in the Look Again section. This could be a nudge to look again at the direction you're moving towards. Are you actually heading the right way?

The Autumn Leaf is squarely in the Clarity section. This could suggest that you need to change and let something go to bring about the clarity you seek.

Taken together, this reading could suggest that you're hiding from taking responsibility for your life and from bringing the dreams you have into reality. It could also indicate that you're simply hoping that things will work out as you'd planned. In fact, though, you need to realign with what's important to you, and then make changes to get what you want.

Interpretation Example 3: Map for Intentions

I created this map to use when you want guidance on how to manifest your intentions.

The map sections include:

- **Dedicate:** charms in this map area identify what you need to dedicate and fully commit to, if you want to bring your intentions into being.
- **Release:** charms that fall here reveal what you need to release to manifest your intentions.
- **Uplevel:** charms in this area give you an idea of where in your life you need to uplevel and raise your standards to align with the energy of your intentions.

- **Focus:** charms in this area show you where you need to focus your time, energy and resources to get what you desire.
- **Nurture:** charms here show you what you need to nurture in yourself or your life to get ready to receive your intention.
- **Receive:** charms in this section reveal what you need to do, be or have to fully receive your intention.

Initial thoughts on this reading:

Looking from a 'wide' perspective first, I yet again notice two main things. First, the charms are clearly split into two. At the top are the Dumbbell, Snail, and Bed charms, while at the bottom are the Jewelled Crown, Hare and Smaller Crown charms. Secondly, there are two clear 'pairs' of charms: the Dumbbell and Snail in one pair, and the Hare and Smaller Crown in the other.

One interpretation of this could be that the top part of the map is about dreaming and aligning with your intention. Meanwhile, the bottom half is about grounding and doing the work to make it happen.

You might also see this as a nudge to slow down (Snail and Bed) and grow stronger (Dumbbell) in your intention, your vision and your why. Meanwhile, you may also need to own your power and sovereignty (Crowns) to create a new beginning (Hare).

A third thing I noticed: at first glance, I totally missed the Palm Trees on the outer ring of the Nurture section. This feels relevant to 'not seeing' what you need to nurture. Are you trying to avoid nurturing something?

Although the Hare is face-down here, I intuitively decided to read it as if it were face-up.

Looking Closer:

The Snail and Dumbbell have both fallen in the centre of the map in the Dedicate section. This may reflect that you need to dedicate time to creating slow, steady, strong foundations. There will be no rushing this intention. You'll need to piece everything together slowly and deliberately.

The Bed is sitting in the Release section. This might mean that you need to rest more and surrender the outcome of this intention over to something bigger than you – for example, Goddess, God or the Universe. Or, alternatively, it could be a nudge to take more focused action.

The Dumbbell is central in this reading. Perhaps this means it's time for strong, clear action such as releasing the Bed (rest) and acting boldly.

The Small Crown and Rabbit both sit in the Focus section. This could be a prompt to use your inner power to get clear on what beginnings you want to create. Or it could refer to getting very clear on your why.

The Jewelled Crown has fallen into the Nurture section. This could mean you need to nurture the sovereignty that you express in the world. Or it could suggest that you need to ask for help, be clear on what you're responsible for and get support where needed. The smaller, plainer crown might feel like the inner work, while the larger, more embellished one might feel more like external energy.

The Palm Trees charm is sitting on the outer ring of Nurture. This might mean you need to stop daydreaming and waiting for the right time or location. In fact, you might need to stop waiting for everything to be 'right' full stop, and just take action.

Finally, the Uplevel and Receive areas are empty. This could be a reassurance that you have everything you need and that everything is as it should be.

This reading could suggest that you need to take slow, steady action to build strong foundations and then act from a place of power and clarity. It could also suggest that you have everything you need right now. So perhaps all you need to do is take clear, aligned action to manifest your intentions.

After Throwing
Your Charms

Recording Your Insights

It can be useful to keep a record of your readings. This practice allows you to look back and see any patterns that are showing up for you. It also helps you to get a broader idea of the themes showing up in your life, and of how the charms speak to you.

Plus, it will help you to deepen your experience with your charms. It can even help you to become more aware of the messages your charms have for you, and how those messages show up in your life.

You may want to keep a note of the following:

- The time and date of the reading
- How you felt before the reading
- The question or guidance that you were after
- The messages you received
- Your intuitive insight
- The overall guidance from traditional symbolism
- Anything that caught your attention more than usual
- Any patterns or pairings of charms that caught your attention

Caring for Your Charms

Although your charms are fairly robust, they still need looking after as part of your sacred toolkit.

Caring for your charms makes them feel more important and special to you. It deepens your respect for them, and your trust in your work with them.

Plus, your charms will benefit from regular cleansing. This clears them of any stagnant energy, and keeps their own energy running free and clear.

It's not essential to cleanse them after every reading, but you'll likely know when they need it. You may find your readings just start to feel 'off', or the charms themselves may feel sticky (either physically or energetically).

If in doubt, give them a cleanse. There are several ways you can do this:

- **Sacred Smoke:** waft your charms gently through some sacred smoke. Alternatively, waft the smoke over your (fireproof) bowl of charms and gently blow the smoke towards the container so that it penetrates your charms.
- **Sacred Sound:** you can pray, sing or play a musical instrument or tuning fork near your charms to cleanse them.
- **Alcohol:** dip your fingers in some kind of alcohol or add a few drops of flower essence to your hands and run your fingers through your charms.
- **Crystals:** place your charms on or near cleansing crystals such as selenite or tourmaline to keep their energy clear.
- **Moonlight:** place your charms on your windowsill on the night of a Full Moon, with the intention that the Full Moon will cleanse and charge your charms.

Of course, if the charms get physically dirty or sticky, cleanse them carefully with rubbing alcohol or running water. Just be mindful of the material your charms are made of: some metals will rust or corrode if they're not dried carefully.

Expanding Your Collection

As you become more confident with using your charms, you'll no doubt be keen to expand your collection. As you do, you can tailor your Charm Casting kit to fit your own personal interests and refine your questioning.

As you collect more charms, you might like to consider the following kinds of objects.

Elements

Perhaps you enjoy working with the elements of Earth, Air, Fire, Water and Spirit.

If so, you could collect pieces that are either made from, or represent, each of the elements.

Then when you ask your questions, you could ask to be shown which element needs attention or is out of balance.

Or you could ask which element to call upon to bring balance or support to the subject of your question.

If these charms fall at the top of your casting area, it could indicate an imbalance in your mental or conscious processes. Or it might mean this element was 'missing' and needed balancing.

Alternatively, if the charms fall at the bottom of your casting area, it might indicate imbalances in your physical self or your unconscious processes. Or it could suggest that this element was too 'dominant' and needed balancing.

Crystals

If you're drawn to working with crystals, you could incorporate them into your readings in several ways.

You could assign an area of your life to particular crystals. Then, when that crystal shows up in your reading, you'd know the area of your life that was asking for attention.

Or you could use a crystal's properties as an indicator of what's needed in relation to your question.

Zodiac

If you're interested in astrology, you could collect charms that represent each of the signs. Or you could include a die with the astrological signs on it, or with the numbers 1-12 to represent the 12 houses.

Then, when one of the charms or the die shows up in your reading, it might represent areas in your life that needed attention.

You could also use these charms to gain more insight into astrological transits in your chart, or the house that you're travelling through.

OR... you could also use them to indicate times or dates in your life. For example, if you wanted some insight into when something was going to start or end, you could interpret a Leo charm as meaning it would happen during the Leo season (around August). Alternatively, you could interpret it as that thing starting or ending when you become more 'Leo': ie. proud, confident, etc.

Chakras

Finally, you could add the seven chakra symbols to your Charm Casting set. Then, as with the crystals, you could use each charm to identify the chakras that need more attention, or are out of balance.

You could do this in a couple of ways.

First, you could interpret the chakra charms, as and when they're cast.

Or you could lay out the seven chakra charms, and then cast your other charms on or around them. Then you could interpret any charms that fall around each chakra as its own reading.

For the second option, you may want to tape or tack down the seven chakra charms, so that they don't scatter around your reading surface. (Of course, you could also interpret their new position as part of the reading, noticing where they move to as an area of imbalance!)

For example, if a chakra charm moved to the right, perhaps you're being too rigid, or need less structure. If it moves to the left, perhaps you need to be less logical… or more creative.

You are only limited by your own imagination!

The SHEro's Journey

The SHEro's Journey Maps

The SHEro's Journey is a path dedicated to women remembering their power and potential as they unapologetically embrace ALL of themselves.

Each stage of the Journey offers its own unique gifts to support you in activating your wisdom, courage, joy and strength. The aim is to help you live an aligned life with clarity and intention.

A shared journey

As you move through your life, it's inevitable that at some point, you'll find yourself at a crossroads. At this moment, you'll be called to make a decision that will likely impact the course of your life. It might be leaving home, starting (or leaving) a job or relationship, or committing to following your dreams.

Each time you make this kind of choice or change, you go through the four stages of the SHEro's Journey:

- The Call
- The Significant Challenge
- The Transformation
- The Return

Find out more about each of these stages on the next few pages.

Sometimes, you'll follow this sequence tidily. At other times though, you may travel back and forth – resisting one phase or not wanting to leave another.

Becoming aware of these stages allows you to step out of confusion, overwhelm and the emotional storms that can accompany change. As a result, you'll experience greater understanding, clarity and a clearer perspective of what you really want and need to do.

Discover where you are on the path

Take the quiz to find out where you are on your SHEro's Journey. Then choose the corresponding Journey Casting Map to explore your experience in more detail. Find the quiz at http://rebeccaanuwen. com/the-quiz/

Stage One: The Call

All great journeys begin with The Call. This is the small voice inside that spurs you to take action. It's probably the voice that originally encouraged you to purchase these charms.

The Call is also the voice telling you that now is the time to make a change and leave the place of 'sameness'. If your soul desires change, you've almost certainly heard The Call.

This stage is exciting. You don't know what lies ahead, so you're caught up in the enthusiasm of the unlimited possibilities that could unfold for you.

However, The Call also brings doubt.

You start out all excited as you listen to your inner voice. Soon, though, you're hearing your mind's chatter: "Oh, maybe I should just leave things as they are?", "Change is always so hard!" or, "I just don't have time!"

Of course, you can decide not to follow The Call during this stage of the journey. That's always a choice.

But you could also carry on, and instead enjoy the adventures of the SHEro's Journey as you dive deep. You could uncover more about yourself, and learn to honour your energy, emotions and feelings.

Just know that whatever path you decide to follow is perfect for you right now.

Stage Two: The Significant Challenge

If you carry on after hearing The Call, you'll experience the next stage of the journey. At the beginning of this stage, you'll meet someone who encourages you. Perhaps they'll offer you a few words of wisdom, or recommend a book or a course that inspires you.

Regardless, you'll feel encouraged enough to commit to your journey and take those first few steps into the unknown.

Once you've made the commitment, however, the Universe often seems to want to see how strong your intentions are. At this point, it can feel as if you're being tested.

During this stage, you'll come face-to-face with people who have all sorts of feelings and opinions about you and the journey you're taking. And not all of those opinions will be supportive.

Some people will try to drag you into their dramas and wear you down with their negative attitudes. They could even leave you wondering why on earth you decided to start your journey when you could've just stayed at home.

When this happens, you may find yourself wondering who you can trust.

Of course, not all of your challenges will take the form of people. Sometimes they'll be situations or projects you're working on. And then there's your inner critic: she'll no doubt have opinions to share with you too.

But mixed in with the naysayers will also be people who fully support what you do. Those people will actively help you on your journey.

Now you'll need to decide who to listen to. You'll also need to select what you'll take with you, and what you'll leave behind.

Whatever you choose, each decision you make teaches you more about yourself.

Stage Three: The Transformation

In the third stage of your journey, you'll approach your biggest obstacle. And at first, you may not realise how hard it will be.

You may feel like you have everything in place, and that the end of your journey – your goal – is in sight. The truth, however, is that you're just part-way along, and about to face the most important test of your journey.

This is where you're likely to feel the most emotion. You may be confronted with aspects of yourself that you'd rather keep hidden. But this is when it's most important to take a long, hard look at yourself.

It's time to take the journey within.

Anything inauthentic that you've been showing to the world is about to crumble away, leaving you with only your True Essence. This may hurt. You may feel vulnerable. Tears are likely – but this is where the real treasure is!

The old you is dying, and the new you is being birthed.

This is a transformation you cannot 'un-experience'. It will forever change you.

And when you come out the other side, you'll view the world around you with fresh eyes, because you've achieved what so many are afraid to do. You've conquered your inner demons, as well as the external naysayers and those who've tried to keep you small. You've been victorious.

It's time to enjoy your accomplishments and rewards.

Stage Four: The Return Home

In the final stage, you've come triumphantly through the inner battle. Now it's time to regroup and continue on.

You're so close to the end of your journey by this stage, but there are still obstacles to trip you up. You may fall again and feel like giving up – it's your long night of the soul.

Yet this is your defining moment. You're determined to complete the journey and return home.

Yes, you could wait to be rescued. But some part of you knows that NOW is the time to invoke your inner SHEro and save yourself. It's time to feel empowered like never before.

You've been strengthened by your successes and failures up to this point. And by pushing through this seemingly dark moment, you can finally break through the limiting beliefs that have been holding you back throughout your life.

For the final time on this particular journey, you have a choice to make.

If you decide to move forward, you'll resolve or satisfy whatever started you on this journey. You'll integrate the knowledge or way of being you've discovered and return home empowered and stronger than before. If you don't – if you resist this final stage – you'll lose the chance to create a deeper connection with yourself and with others (at least for this time around).

Either way, it's time to complete your journey and return home.

And either way, you've changed. You're not the same woman who started this journey.

It's time to live your life for you.

It's time to live your life on your terms.

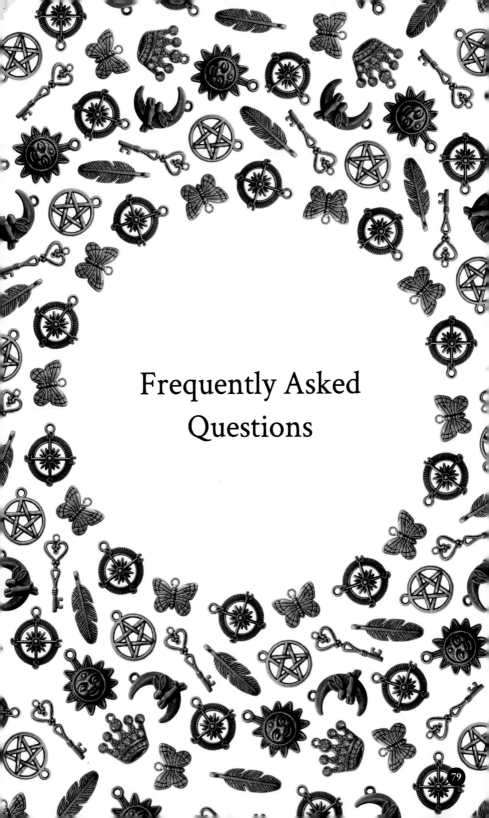

Frequently Asked Questions

What can I ask my charms?

You can ask your charms anything.

No topic is off-limits. You just need to be open to receiving the answers.

I'd recommend sticking with open-ended questions though, rather than 'Yes' / 'No' questions.

'Yes / No' questions can be limiting, whereas open-ended questions give you the opportunity to explore your thoughts and feelings around a particular subject.

For example, the Yes/No question, "Will I get this job?" is very limiting in terms of the useful information it gives you. Try instead asking an open-ended question like, "What will be the outcome of getting the job?" Or, as an alternative, "What do I need to focus on to improve my chances of getting a job that supports my vision of the future?"

Is there a process I must follow when I cast my charms?

No, there's no strict process to follow. As we've talked about in this book, there's no one 'right' way to work with your charms.

You will, however, quickly find your own favourite way of using them.

Remember that these are your charms, so however you work with them will be perfect for you. It may not look like the way other people use their charms, and that's perfectly OK.

That said, I always suggest taking a moment to pause and get clear on the question you want to ask. Sometimes, that question might just be, "What charm do I need for general guidance in my life right now?"

A clear question gives you a better chance of getting a clear answer.

How often can I use my charms?

Use your charms as often as you want to.

Sometimes I use mine multiple times a day. During other times, I don't use them for a couple of weeks.

Again, they're your charms, so you get to decide how often you want to use them.

Just remember that they're a tool to gain access to your inner wisdom. They don't replace or override that inner wisdom.

How many charms can I cast at once?

When you start out on your Charm Casting adventure, I suggest casting around 8-12 charms, but you can start with much fewer, perhaps even just 1-5. When you start small, it's easier to connect with the answers. If you start with too many before you get confident, you can easily overwhelm yourself.

In the same way, I recommend starting simple with your casting surface. You could even cast your first charms onto a blank surface. That way, the only things you're thinking about will be the charms themselves, their meanings and their relationships to each other.

As you become more experienced, you can start to add more layers into your readings with growing confidence. Remember, we all had to crawl and stumble before we could walk and then run. This skill is no different.

What if I can't think of a meaning for a charm?

If you can't identify a meaning for one of the charms, you're likely overthinking it. You're probably trying to get it 'right', rather than get it right for you.

When you find yourself feeling stuck, pause and take a breath. Close your eyes, then re-open them and look at the charm with fresh eyes.

Think about what you associate with the charm, and ask yourself:

What feelings does it bring up?

What experiences have you had with whatever the charm represents?

How do you feel about those experiences?

Has the charm come up for you before? If so, what did it represent then?

If you still feel blocked, leave the charm where it is, and go and do something else. Come back to it later, and see what message you get from it this time.

Finally, if you still can't connect with the charm, make a note of it and put it back in your container. Then simply pick another one.

I say 'make a note of it' because it might represent something you're blocking or refusing to face, or something that's not ready to come through yet. Or, of course, you may also just have been having that kind of day!

Can I get the interpretation of the reading wrong?

No. Charm Casting is connecting with your intuition. You have the final say on what your charms mean. It doesn't have to make sense to anyone else. It only has to resonate with you.

However, I do have one caveat... you're connecting with your intuition, which will NEVER speak badly or negatively to you. It will NEVER ask you to cause harm to yourself or others.

So if you receive a negative message (and I don't simply mean uncomfortable - sometimes growth is uncomfortable – but negative towards yourself or someone else), that's not your intuition. In that case, it's your ego, doubts or fears.

Your intuition isn't all 'love and light', but it's also not harmfully destructive.

Can the meaning of a charm change?

Yes, it can.

Most of your charms will probably keep their same meaning. However, as you go through life, you'll have more life experiences – change, growth, loss, joy, love, etc. And the meanings of some of your charms may evolve to reflect this new understanding, wisdom and experience.

In other words, as you change, so does the meaning you give to life events. This can then be reflected in any meanings you give your charms.

Charms may also have different meanings in a reading depending on where they sit relative to other charms.

For example, a Caged Bird may represent somewhere secure and safe for you to express yourself and sing your own song. But if you cast the Caged Bird charm near something restrictive, such as a Handcuffs, Belt or Sword charm, your interpretation may be that the bird is being limited, and should be set free.

Can I look up the symbolic meaning of a charm?

While you can look up the traditional symbolism of whatever the charm represents, your own interpretation will always be more accurate.

Remember that there's no wrong way to interpret your charms.

Your meaning for a charm may be different from someone else's and that's always OK. Your life experience and beliefs are different from that person's, so of course you're likely to interpret your charms differently.

Once more, these are your charms. They help you connect with YOUR intuition. This is a journey towards trusting yourself. If you find yourself seeking lots of guidance from others, or from guidebooks etc., pause for a moment. Ask yourself why you think other people have the answers, and you don't.

Again, you can't get it wrong. You don't need validation from anyone else.

This is your relationship with yourself, so you get to have the final say.

Can I make my own guidebook?

I love the idea of making your own guidebook.

You could make a guidebook to record how different charms, or even combinations of charms, show up for you. But again, remember that even if you're the one who wrote it, it's only a guide – your own interpretations may change over time as you do.

That said, creating your own guidebook would be a great way to develop and deepen your experience with your charms.

Do I need to cleanse my charms?

All sacred tools that you use regularly benefit from cleansing to clear them of any stagnant energy and keep their own energy running free and clear. Also, caring for your charms makes them feel more important and special to you. It deepens your respect for them, and your trust in your work with them.

See the Caring for Your Charms section of this book on page [insert page number of "Caring for Your Charms"] for ideas on how to cleanse your charms.

Do I need to have a specific spiritual practice for the charms to work?

Not at all.

You can follow any spiritual practice or religion (or none at all) and still work with your charms. When you work with charms, you're simply deepening your connection to your own inner wisdom and intuition.

You're not calling in anything or anyone external, unless that's in accordance with your own practices. While you can invoke a particular deity in Charm Casting if you want to, it's certainly not a requirement.

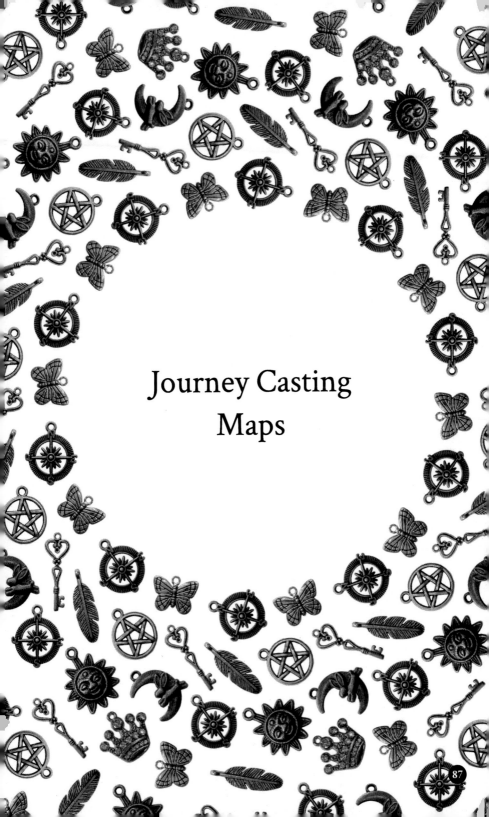

Journey Casting
Maps

MAP FOR CHANGE

First Steps

Commit

Review

Change

Do Differently

Release

Overcome

MAP FOR CLARITY

Avoiding

Look Again

Hidden

Clarity

MAP FOR INTENTIONS

Receive

Nurture

Dedicate

Focus

Release

Uplevel

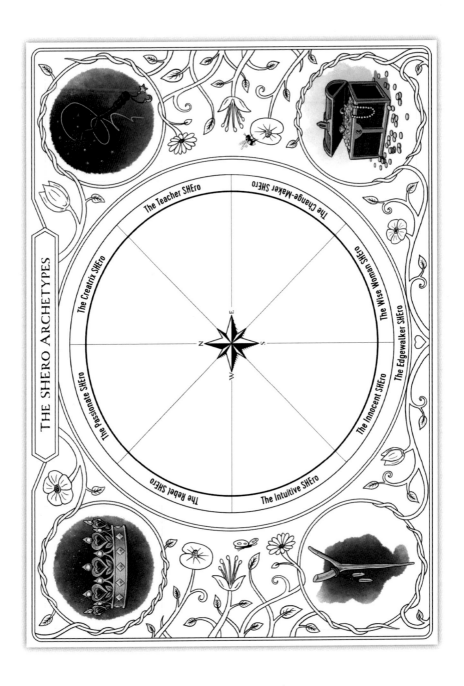

THE SHERO ARCHETYPES

The Teacher SHEro
The Change-Maker SHEro
The Creatrix SHEro
The Wise Woman SHEro
The Edgewalker SHEro
The Passionate SHEro
The Innocent SHEro
The Rebel SHEro
The Intuitive SHEro

THE CALL - MAKE A CHOICE

Focus On
Embrace
Growth
Trust
Accept
Reflect
Align
Support

THE SIGNIFICANT CHALLENGE - TAKE ACTION

Bold Action
Push Through
Commit
Let Go
Obstacles Unseen
Celebrate
Obstacles Seen

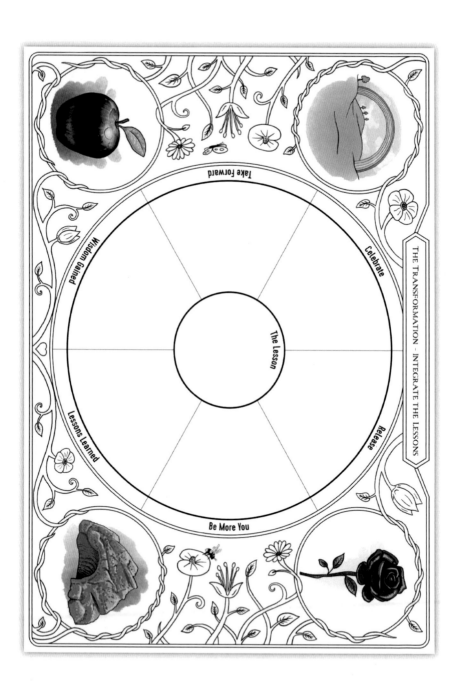

THE TRANSFORMATION - INTEGRATE THE LESSONS

The Lesson

Take Forward

Celebrate

Release

Be More You

Lessons Learned

Wisdom Gained

THE RETURN - EMBODY YOUR TRUTH

Speak Up

Reclaim

Express

Remember

Take Up Space

Unapologetic

Notes

Notes

Notes

Manufactured by Amazon.ca
Bolton, ON

34946597R00062